MPJE®

Federal Pharmacy Law Review

2nd Edition

Eric Christianson, PharmD, BCPS, BCGP

MPJE® Master: Federal Pharmacy Law Review

Copyright © 2023 by Eric Christianson, Pharm.D., BCPS, BCGP

Introduction

If you are like most pharmacists or pharmacy students, you enjoy taking care of patients, identifying drug therapy problems, and making a difference by using your expert knowledge about medications. Unfortunately, having a basic understanding of laws, regulations, and regulatory agencies that impact the profession is a necessary evil. If you cannot pass the state law exam (MPJE), you can't work as a pharmacist and do all the really cool things that you've wanted to do (including pay off your student loans).

MPJE Master: Federal Pharmacy Law Review was intended to simplify the process of learning pharmacy law. We've outlined critical components of federal pharmacy law that you will need to know to pass your MPJE exam. I was always the student in school that needed to highlight the most important information to remember and then I would memorize that information.

Recalling information from a large textbook was always difficult for me. Rather than reading a textbook, we've supplied the information in easily digestible, bite-sized pieces. We've used bullet points to help you be able to quickly memorize important facts about each agency, regulation, law, etc.

We've also created a helpful list of questions within the book to help you identify areas of pharmacy practice where state laws can often vary. This table is a list of questions that you can fill in as you read your respective states' laws and regulations. We've added this to ensure that you don't overlook the important differences in pharmacy laws across the United States.

Whether you are a new graduate who needs to pass your law exam to begin your practice or a 20-year veteran who is moving to a new state, this review will absolutely help prepare you to pass your MPJE law exam and help you obtain your pharmacy license.

Table of Contents

Food and Drug Administration (FDA) and Related Agencies

Food and Drug Administration

- Agency within the United States Federal Government
- Became the consumer protection agency with regard to food and drugs with the 1906 Pure Food and Drugs Act
- The most important agency when it comes to approving companies to market and sell their drugs to the public
- Responsibilities include:
  - Protecting public health
  - Ensuring safety and efficacy of drugs (veterinary and human products)
  - Ensuring safety and efficacy of biologic medications
  - Ensuring safety and efficacy of medical devices
  - Ensuring safety of cosmetics

     ○   Ensuring safety of food supply (supplements fall under this category)

Center for Drug Evaluation and Research (CDER)

- Task: Ensure that safe and effective drugs are available to improve the health of patients and not pose unreasonable risks
  - Phase 1 clinical trials
    - Phase 1 involves giving the drug (or medical device) to humans for the first time
    - Given to a small number (few dozen to no more than 100) of healthy volunteers
    - In general, these patients are younger and do not necessarily have the disease that the drug is intended to treat
    - Important for gathering what effects the drug will have on humans
    - Pharmacokinetics (absorption, distribution, metabolism, and elimination) data is also important in this phase

- Doses are escalated and patients are monitored for effects of the drug
- It is estimated that 70% of drugs pass through this phase successfully
  - Phase 2
    - First time that a drug's efficacy is tested in humans
    - Given to patients who have the actual disease
    - 100's of patients usually involved in testing, but less than 1,000
    - Randomized controlled trials are typically first done in this phase where a control group is set up to receive standard of care or placebo; side effects and tolerability are also monitored
  - Phase 3
    - Larger clinical trials that will often encompass up to 3,000 patients
    - Trials can be done across the country/world (multi-centered)
    - Monitor new drug for safety and efficacy
    - Final phase prior to approval of the drug for sale to the general public

- - Identify specific dosing and indication, which provides much of the information for the package insert and labeling of the drug
  - Phase 4
    - Often referred to as Post-Marketing Surveillance
    - FDA/CDER continues to track and monitor a medication for safety and efficacy following approval of release to the general public
    - Drug is being used in clinical practice, possibly given to tens of thousands of patients or more
    - Rare side effects may be identified in Phase 4 monitoring
    - Long term use data can be better understood
- Investigation New Drug (IND) Application
  - Asking for permission to give a new drug or product to humans
  - Prior to Phase 1 clinical trials
- New Drug Application (NDA)
  - Seeking approval of a new drug to be able to sell the drug to the general public
  - The drug company or sponsor presents clinical trial information to the FDA for potential approval for sale

- 10 Types of NDAs
    - Type 1: New Molecular Entity – Active ingredient that has never been previously approved
    - Type 2: New Active Ingredient – This is a drug that has been approved but a new salt, ester, or other formulation has been created and is seeking FDA approval
    - Type 3: New Dosage Form – Previously approved active ingredient but a manufacturer has created a new dosage form for approval
    - Type 4: New Combination – Previously approved medications seeking approval to be used in a single combination dosage form
    - Type 5: New Formulation – This NDA type is a catch all for any unique formulation change (other than new dosage form – Type 3); an example may be changes to the inactive ingredients of a product that would require performing clinical studies
    - Type 6: – Retired classification; replaced by Type 9 and Type 10
    - Type 7: – Previously marketed drug without an approved NDA (think grandfathered medications)
    - Type 8: Prescription to OTC switch

- o Type 9: New Indication or Claim with the drug not to be marketed
- o Type 10: New indication or Claim with the drug to be marketed after approval
- Abbreviated New Drug Application (ANDA)
  - o Approval process for a generic medication
  - o Bioequivalence is the only thing that needs to be proven
  - o Generic manufacturers do not need to do all the clinical testing that the original company who did the NDA has to do
- Supplemental New Drug Application (SNDA)
  - o Formal application submitted by a drug manufacturer to the FDA for approval of changes in packaging, labeling, dosages, etc.
  - o In order to submit an SNDA, the drug must already have been approved by the FDA under a previously existing NDA
  - o The drug manufacturer must submit evidence to support the change
- Over-the-Counter approval
  - o The FDA approves medications to be sellable to consumers without the supervision of a physician
- Fast track designation

- A company may petition the FDA for "Fast track" approval of their drug
- If the drug treats a serious or lethal condition and it is a novel agent that meets a need that has not been met by currently available FDA approved agents, it is more likely to receive this designation
- Example; a drug that has been shown to cure HIV would likely get fast track approval

FDA Classification

- P Drugs
  - FDA chooses this classification when a drug is a novel treatment or has advantages over existing treatments
  - This type of drug will receive special attention and be approved more quickly
  - Another way to think about a P-classification would be to recognize that the FDA would have a "priority" review
- S Drugs
  - This classification is selected by the FDA for drugs that have a similar molecule to an already approved FDA drug

- S class of drug basically represents a "Me Too" drug, i.e. a new PPI
- These drugs would receive a "standard" type review and the FDA would not be in a hurry to approve the drug

Right to Try Legislation

- Legislation that allows patients with life-threatening diseases or conditions who have tried every FDA approved agent to utilize agents that have made it through Phase 1 testing but are not currently approved (remember that it takes completing all three phases to get approval)

Center for Biologics Evaluation and Research (CBER)

- FDA controlled institution
- Responsible for the approval of biologic medications
- Focus on safety and efficacy for biologic agents, analogous to what the CDER does for traditional medications

- Biologic License Application (BLA) is the application submitted by a company to get their biologic product approved for sale in the United States (similar to a New Drug Application for traditional medications)

MedWatch

- Under the FDA umbrella
- Helps ensure safety of medications by allowing patients, consumers, and healthcare professionals the ability to report serious adverse reactions or problems with medications, biologics, devices, or dietary supplements
- Form 3500B can be utilized by patients and non-healthcare professionals to report adverse events
- Form 3500 is the form utilized by healthcare professionals
- Reporting of adverse reactions or problems to MedWatch is NOT mandatory

FDA Drug Recalls

- Class 1
    - Highest risk, most urgent

- o Possibility exists for immediate danger, death, or serious injury
- o It is rare for this type of recall to happen
- o Action should be taken ASAP when the individual/pharmacy becomes aware of the recall
- o Drugs need to be prevented from reaching the patient
- o Contact with patient is necessary to ensure that the patient does not utilize the product
- Class 2
  - o No immediate danger
  - o Risk of injury is possible, but unlikely to be serious
  - o Injury or adverse effects that do occur will most likely be temporary or reversible with cessation of the product
- Class 3
  - o No immediate danger with use of the product
  - o Often used when a product has not met the FDA rules and regulations
  - o Example – non-harmful substance found in a drug product

Orange Book

- A formal list of all FDA approved drugs including OTCs
- Mandated by the Hatch-Waxman amendments
- This reference is used to identify which medications can be substituted for one another
- AB rated drugs are those that are classified as therapeutically equivalent and can be substituted for one another
- Some drugs will contain AB ratings with different numbers; typically, in situations where they are two or more medications that have the same drug, strength, and dosage form but are not bioequivalent
  - Diltiazem is a good example
  - One generic formulation may have a rating of AB3 which would indicate that it matches the same product with the AB3 rating
  - An AB2 rated generic product would not be acceptable to substitute for an AB3 product or vice versa
- Other ratings that are utilized in the Orange Book:
  - AA No bioequivalence problems in conventional dosage forms

- AN refers to an aerosolized solution or powder
- AO refers to oil solutions that can be injected
- AP refers to aqueous solutions
- AT refers to topical products
- Any designation that starts with a B is indicative of two agents that cannot be substituted for one another, they are not therapeutically equivalent

Purple Book

- Analogous to the Orange Book except that it is a list of biologic drugs
- Identifies agents that are considered to be biosimilar agents

Legislation Impacting Pharmacy

Biologics Control Act of 1902

- Ensured safety and purity of vaccines, serums, and products that were used to treat or prevent diseases

Pure Food and Drug Act of 1906

- Prohibited interstate commerce of misbranded and adulterated drugs

1938 Food, Drug, and Cosmetic Act (FDCA)

- New drugs must be proven safe before marketing
- Factory inspections allowed

- Provided safe tolerances be set for unavoidable poisonous substances

Durham-Humphrey Amendment of 1951

- Defines which drugs can and cannot be safely used without medical supervision and requires that a patient have a prescription from a licensed practitioner before being allowed to purchase certain medications(OTC versus prescription)

Kefauver-Harris Amendment of 1962

- Legislation that ensured efficacy and safety of a medication were proven prior to being sold and marketed
- Added following the discovery of thalidomide causing birth defects

Poison Prevention Packaging Act (PPPA) - 1970

- Protects children from accidentally ingesting harmful chemicals and prescription medication
- Requires that drugs need to have childproof containers
- Requires that poisonous chemicals, cleaners, etc. have safety packaging that would prevent dangerous access for kids
  - There are exceptions, usually medications that may require quick access, like nitroglycerin
- Blister packs are ok and do not fall under this requirement (it would take a long time for kids to ingest a significant quantity)
- Elderly patients or patients with disorders that impact dexterity and strength may struggle to open the childproof caps
  - Patients can request "no childproof caps" on all prescriptions
  - Pharmacies will typically require the request to be in writing to protect themselves from liability
  - A provider may request a one-time fill with a non-childproof bottle but CANNOT sign a blanket waiver for all medications

Medical Device Amendment of 1976

- Held medical devices up to a higher safety and efficacy standard
- Legislation was stimulated by a report of thousands of injuries due to intrauterine devices in women
- Three classes of medical devices were set up
  - Class 1 – Lower risk devices where significant injury or death is unlikely
  - Class 2 – Moderate risk
  - Class 3 – High risk of significant injury or death

Tamper Resistant Packing Regulation of 1982

- Made it a crime to tamper with packaged consumer products
- This legislation was brought about by an individual who placed cyanide tablets in a Tylenol bottle

Orphan Drug Act of 1983

- Enabled FDA to promote research for drugs needed for rare diseases
- Incentivized manufacturers to create new medications for conditions affecting less than 200,000 people (i.e. the new medication is unlikely to be profitable)
- Incentives to manufacturers include waived FDA fees, tax credits, bonus market exclusivity

Hatch-Waxman Act (Drug Price Competition and Patent Term Restoration Act)

- Created the generic drug system that we have today
- Made it easier for generic manufacturers to get into the market and drive down the costs of medications
- The Abbreviated New Drug Application became easier with passage of this legislation
- Ensured market exclusivity for a period of time for the innovator of the new drug

- Simplified the process by requiring that generic drug makers only need to prove bioequivalence

Prescription Drug Marketing Act (1987-1988)

- Required licensing of wholesalers
- Restricts reimportation
- Bans sale, trade, and purchase of drug samples
- Bans diversion of prescription drugs from standard, legitimate commercial channels

Dietary Supplement Health and Education Act (DSHEA) – 1994

- Classifies dietary supplements as "food"
- Authorizes FDA to promote that good manufacturing processes should apply to dietary supplements (in addition to prescription medications)
- FDA has a more retroactive role
  - Relies on information/concerns from consumers and healthcare professionals

- o Supplements should not be misbranded or adulterated; FDA has authority to take legal action against a company
- o Supplements do not need to go through the FDA clinical trial phases to be able to be sold and marketed
- o Manufacturers do not have to prove that they are safe prior to selling/marketing
- o Specific claims cannot be made about treating, curing, diagnosing, or alleviating symptoms of illnesses
- o Must be labeled as a "dietary supplement" or similar term (herbal, vitamin, etc.)

Health Insurance Portability and Accountability Act (HIPAA) - 1996

- Provides standards for handling patient information
- Protects privacy of patient medical and health related information
- Also focuses on maintaining appropriate access of information for healthcare professionals to adequately do their job
- No restrictions on use or release of de-identified health information

FDA Modernization Act of 1997

- Regulated advertising of unapproved (off-label) uses of drugs
- Created opportunities for speedier, "fast track", reviews of new medications to shorten the approval process of medications for life-threatening and serious conditions
- Increased requirements for studies in children if the drug was likely to be used in this patient population

Medicare Prescription Drug Improvement and Modernization Act of 2003

- Medicare part D prescription benefit created
  - Implemented in 2006

The Affordable Care Act of 2010 (AKA Obamacare)

- Numerous provisions impacting patients, insurance companies, and healthcare professionals
- Allowed provisions impacting patients, insurance companies, and healthcare professionals
- Allowed "older children" to remain on their parents' healthcare plan until age 26
- Attempted to reduce insurance companies selecting to cover only healthy patients
- Established the CMS Innovation Center to experiment/test various healthcare delivery models to try to maximize service and minimize cost
    - MTM model was one of those models to receive expanded testing

The Inflation Reduction Act

- Provisions within this legislation cap the cost of insulin at 35$ for patients under Medicare Part D
- Enhances vaccine utilization by ensuring that copays are eliminated for Medicare patients

Vaccines for Children Program

- Federally funded program that provides 16 vaccinations at no cost to children who may not be able to afford it
- CDC purchases the vaccines at a reduced price and sends them to individual state department of health agencies

Agencies Impacting Pharmacy

OSHA (Occupational Safety and Health Administration)

- Focused on protection of healthcare workers who may be exposed to hazardous drugs, blood borne pathogens, etc.
  - Chemo is the classic medication hazard example
- OSHA sets standards for use of toxic medications
  - Looks at safety and procedures including:
    - Handling
    - Administration
    - Storage
    - Disposal
    - Transportation
- OSHA standards include oversight of MSDS information - see below

Material Safety Data Sheets

- Now called SDS (safety data sheets)
- OSHA requires that all employers who use, store, transfer, etc. hazardous substances to provide employees access to the safety data sheets for each given substance
- Manufacturers are required to provide information on how to handle, transfer, use and appropriately store potentially hazardous substances
- Chemotherapy agents will often be a hazardous substance and employees will need access to the information (SDS) if requested
- Important information contained within SDS of a drug/hazardous substance
    - Name of chemical compound
    - What to do if there is inappropriate exposure
    - Procedures for accidents with the drug/substance
    - Risks associated with exposure or inappropriate use (corrosive, difficulty breathing if inhaled, flammable, etc.)
    - What type of protective equipment needs to be used

NIOSH (National Institute for Occupation Safety and Health)

- NIOSH drug list is important to pharmacists
- List of hazardous drugs that may impact the health and safety of healthcare professionals who administer, compound, or dispense these medications
- Possible risks from exposure to these hazardous agents include developmental issues, reproductive concerns, and carcinogenicity
- Oncology and hormonal agents are two categories of drugs that often fall into the NIOSH list
- Drugs on the NIOSH list need to be handled with special care
- Special precautions when utilizing these drugs might include wearing Personal Protective Equipment (PPE)

Environmental Protection Agency (EPA)

- Defines hazardous waste and recommends processes for appropriate disposal of these type of agents

- Hazardous waste must meet 1 of the following categories (TIRC)
    - T - Toxic - harmful to people when ingested
    - I - Ignitability - ability to start on fire/combust
    - R - Reactivity - ability to cause/start a chemical reaction that may be harmful or dangerous
    - C - Corrosive - anything with a very high or low pH that can cause damage to skin and other human tissue when contacted
- Many drugs and chemicals that are used in healthcare are considered hazardous wastes
- P-listed drugs - special disposal is recommended
    - Common examples: warfarin and nicotine
    - To be considered waste, it must contain a P-listed chemical (i.e. warfarin, nicotine, etc.), and be in the unused form and be a commercial product
- The EPA recognizes the importance of preventing pharmaceutical agents from getting into the environment
- Patients are encouraged to take medications back to a local sheriff's office, pharmacy

where a take-back program is available, or other events where unused pharmaceuticals are being collected by an authorized agency

- If taking drugs back is not an option, the EPA has the following guidelines for household disposal:
    - Remove drugs from the vial
    - Combine the drugs with kitty litter or coffee grounds
    - Put contents in a container that can be closed (i.e. Ziploc bag, container with a lid)
    - Remove or black out HIPAA information from the empty vials
    - Place in trash

Division of Medication Error Prevention and Analysis (DMEPA)

- Under the umbrella of the Center for Drug Evaluation and Research (CDER)
- Reviews medication error reports on prescription and OTC drugs
- The National Coordinating Council for Medication Error Reporting and Prevention defines a medication error as, "any preventable event that may cause or lead to inappropriate medication use or patient harm while the medication is in the control of the

health care professional, patient, or consumer. Such events may be related to professional practice, health care products, procedures, and systems, including prescribing, order communication, product labeling, packaging, nomenclature, compounding, dispensing, distribution, administration, education, monitoring, and use."

- They work closely with Institute of Safe Medicine Practices (ISMP) and United States Pharmacopeia (USP)

ISMP Medication Errors Reporting Program (MERP)

- VOLUNTARY, confidential reporting of medication errors
- Reports are forwarded to the FDA
- ISMP may also send on to manufacturers as appropriate
  - I.e. look alike labeling or sound alike medications that can lead to healthcare professionals making errors
  - Can report good catches
- Medication Errors
  - Medication errors can lead to patient distress, injury, disability, or death

- o Errors with high risk medications are very concerning
    - ▪ Examples: warfarin and other anticoagulants, insulin, seizure medications
- o Reporting of errors should be encouraged to monitor for trends, recognize potential safety concerns when administering, dispensing, or ordering medications, and identify areas for targeted education
- Develop a culture of safety ("Just Culture")
    - o Emphasis on creating a system focused on patient safety
    - o Healthcare institutions will never be perfect with humans involved in patient care, but they should strive for continuous improvement
    - o Looks at work environment and processes to ensure that processes aren't contributing to the potential risk of a healthcare professional making an error

ISMP Vaccine Errors Reporting Program (VERP)

- VOLUNTARY
- Vaccine reporting only

- Reporting of vaccine errors and good catches

VAERS (Vaccine Adverse Event Reporting System)

- It is for vaccines that have been approved and are currently on the market
- Report non-preventable adverse reactions
- They analyze the data reported
- Play a significant role in surveillance
  - Typically, rare events that may not be very detectable in research trials
- Makes adverse reaction information available to the public
- NOT mandatory
- Part of Department of Health and Human Services

National Institute of Health (NIH)

- US government agency for biomedical research
- Part of Department of Health and Human Services
- Funds clinical trials through taxpayer dollars

- Tries to expand knowledge base of biomedical community
- Improve the health of the public through research efforts

Institute of Medicine

- Responsible for "To Err is Human" report
  o Shed light on medication and healthcare associated errors
  o Put focus on system improvement versus blaming healthcare professionals or individuals

Agency for Healthcare Quality and Research (AHQR)

- Create evidence to improve healthcare by making it safer, better, equitable, more accessible, and affordable
- Under the Department of Health and Human Services
- Focuses on the healthcare system as a whole
- Helps create and support methods and training programs that save lives

Nation Quality Forum (NQF)

- Focus on the healthcare system as a whole
- Helps create and support methods and training programs that save lives
- Endorses healthcare standards/quality measures
- Recommends which quality measure should be used in payment and public reporting programs
- Example measures
  - 30-day post hospital acute MI discharge care transition
  - Comprehensive diabetes care
    - Blood pressure goals, eye exam, A1C control, cholesterol management
  - Severe sepsis and septic shock
- Provides reports and various tools to help providers and other healthcare professionals stay on top of quality improvement and quality standards

Office of Prescription Drug Promotion (OPDP)

- Monitors prescription medication advertising

- Primary responsibilities include ensuring that advertising is balanced, truthful, and not misleading

Centers for Medicare and Medicaid (CMS)

CMS

- Part of the Department of Health and Human Services
- Administers the following healthcare programs
  - Medicare
  - Medicaid
  - Health Insurance Marketplace
- Patients become eligible for Medicare coverage when they turn age 65 or have a disability, ESRD, or ALS

Medicare Part A

- Hospital benefits
- Will cover care in a skilled nursing facility under certain circumstances

Medicare part B

- Coverage includes:
  - Clinic and preventative care benefits
  - Durable medical equipment
  - Nebulizers and nebulized medications, diabetic testing supplies, and drugs delivered by pumps
  - Most vaccines
  - Drugs for ESRD may be covered

Medicare part C

- Often called Medicare Advantage Plans
- A premium, private insurance plan approved by CMS that incorporates more benefits than what Medicare part A and B provide
- Additional benefits that may fall under Medicare Part C include prescription drugs, vision, and dental
- Typically, more expensive than traditional Medicare due to some of the additional benefits

Medicare part D

- Outpatient dispensing pharmacy benefit
- New enrollees have 7 months to sign up during the initial enrollment period
- Plans will have multiple tiers for drug coverage
- Tier 1 - little to no copay, most often generic medications will fall into this category
- Tier 2 - preferred brand name medications are found in this category, they will cost more than Tier 1, but significantly less than non-preferred brand name meds
- Tier 3 - non-preferred brand name medications that are generally more expensive
- Specialty Tier - specialty drugs (i.e. biologics); often the most expensive medications for patients
- Uniquely, Shingrix (Zoster Vaccine - Recombinant, Adjuvanted) is covered under part D while most others are covered under part B
- Donut hole - when the patient and drug plan spends a specific amount of money, there is a time when the patient must pay the entire amount for the medication before the insurance company kicks in and starts paying again

- The donut hole has been phased out as of 2020 and no longer exists - this phasing out of the donut hole was part of the Affordable Care Act legislation of 2010
- There does remain a "coverage gap" where beneficiaries will pay up to 25% of the cost of the drug when a certain spending threshold is met
- In 2023, that spending threshold amount is $4,660
- Drugs that are typically not covered by part D include: benzodiazepines, weight loss/weight gain drugs, OTCs, barbiturates, fertility, and hair growth drugs
- Protected drug classes - a group of 6 drug classes that insurers must cover the majority or all medications within that class to ensure adequate access for patients
  - Seizure drugs
  - Antidepressants
  - Antipsychotics
  - Oncology
  - HIV
  - Immunosuppressants

Medicare Record Keeping

- Prescription records must be kept for a 10-year period

- With computerization, most pharmacies will have them on record indefinitely

Medigap

- Type of coverage provided by a private insurer that helps pay for out of pocket expenses that are not covered by Medicare
- Typically, this includes co-payments, deductibles and other costs from Medicare part A and part B that are not paid for by the plan
- This type of insurance generally does not cover the "donut hole" of part D plans

CMS Innovation Center

- Intention was to reduce cost of care by testing innovative payment and service delivery models to help reduce expenses
- Evaluates service delivery models and tries to identify best practices and lessons learned from each tested payment and service delivery model

Medication Therapy Management Benefit

- Benefit provided through Medicare Part D
- Requires THREE specific criteria be met for patients to be eligible for MTM benefit (drug spend is usually the limiting factor)
    - Annual drug spend of at least X amount of dollars (set annually, usually in the $4,000-$5,000 range)
    - Minimum of 2 or 3 chronic diseases
    - Minimum of 2-8 Part D covered medications
- Billing codes
    - 99605 – initial 15 minutes for a new patient
    - 99606 – initial 15 minutes for an established patient
    - 99607 – subsequent 15 minutes regardless of new or established patient
- Example Billing: Met with an established patient for 45 minutes
    - Bill 1 unit – 99606 and bill 2 units of 99607

Comprehensive Medication Review (CMR)

- MTM program benefit through Medicare part D which is delivered from the community/retail pharmacy; requirements include:
  - Interactive person to person, telehealth, or phone medication review (cannot be done as a medical record review)
  - Helps to improve the patient's knowledge of their medications
  - Assess medication therapies, including OTC, prescription, and herbal medications
  - Identify and create a list of medication problems
  - Create a plan to fix those problems with the patient, caregiver, or provider
- CMR documentation also follows a general format. The recommended format is;
  - CMR Cover Letter (CL)
  - Medication Action Plan (MAP)
  - Personal Medication List (PML)
- CMR can be provided and billed annually

Targeted Medication Review

- Part of the MTM program that is designed to enhance follow up and monitoring of patient medication use
- Usually less intensive than a CMR; it may be done for a specific reason such as, a patient reports new problems, a new medication is started, or there is a transition in care
- Can be done and billed quarterly

Risk Evaluation and Mitigation Strategy (REMS)

- Goal: Ensure the benefits of the drug is greater than the risk
- Used for certain drugs that pose higher risks
- Goes above and beyond usual labeling
- Strictness of the program will depend upon the perceived risk of the medications
- Classic examples of medications that have a REMS program:
  - Accutane (isotretinoin) - iPLEDGE
  - Clozaril (clozapine) - online registry
- Drug sponsor develops the REMS program
  - FDA reviews and approves it

- Can be required for a class of drugs or an individual drug
- May be required by the FDA before approval of an investigational new drug or the FDA may require it because of information reviewed from post-marketing surveillance (phase 4 of clinical monitoring)
- REMS for new drugs and biologics need to have a timetable for assessment
  - At times of assessment, the REMS may be eliminated or revised if data has been positive in demonstrating that the risk of the drug is not that significant
- REMS Medication Guides
  - Written in patient friendly language
  - Given to patient when dispensing the medication
  - Not intended to replace standard patient education, but given in addition to the usual patient education handouts

Elements to Assure Safe Use (ETASU) – part of the REMS program

- Required tasks for healthcare professionals

- Done prior to prescribing or dispensing
- Most involve labor-intensive work for the healthcare professional
- Examples:
  - Specialized training
  - Drug to be given in a certain setting only (i.e. hospital)
  - Lab tests may need to be done prior to dispensing/prescribing

Accountable Care Organization

- Directly from the CMS website, "an ACO is a group of physicians, hospitals and other healthcare professionals who come together voluntarily to commit to provide high quality and highly coordinated care to Medicare patients"
- An ACO is focused on coordination of care
- Attempt to minimize excessive care and ultimately save money
- Duplicate labs and services, and providing low level care in an emergency department or hospital is an inappropriate use of resources and is what an ACO seeks to help minimize
- Ideally, an ACO seeks to improve quality, cost effectiveness, and provide total care for a patient

Managed Care, Healthcare Institutions, and Research

IRB (Institutional Review Board)

- Committee used in research that is responsible for approving, monitoring, and reviewing biomedical research
- Protect the rights and welfare of human research participants
- IRB will review protocols and planned research process as well as materials given to patients (i.e. informed consent, patient education that explains the proposed research study)
- An IRB needs to register with Health and Human Services if doing FDA regulated studies
- An institution doesn't have to its own IRB, it can have an outside IRB
- IRB members can be paid, reimbursed for expenses, etc.

- Potential conflicts of interest should be considered when selecting members for an IRB
- Expedited review - IRB can use this to approve and review minor changes in already previously approved research (completed by IRB chairperson or one of the experienced members appointed by chairperson)
- Informed consent is not required for children; however, many consider it standard practice to obtain informed consent from older children who understand the circumstances surrounding the research
- IRB should be composed of at least 5 members with varying backgrounds to assure appropriate review of research activities
  - Cannot contain only one profession
  - Every effort shall be made to have a mix of men and women who are qualified to serve
  - Shall contain at least one member who works primarily in scientific areas and one member who focuses on non-scientific areas
  - Conflicts of interest would not be allowed in members of the IRB
    - One member shall not be affiliated with the institution or have an immediate family member who is affiliated with the institution

Conflicts of Interest (ethics)

- Major concern is in drug research
  - Concern with an investigator or other individual involved in a clinical trial who may have a financial interest in the company that is making the drug being investigated
- All persons with potential conflicts of interest should disclose such relationships prior to being involved in a study or clinical research
- Multiple changes/alterations in study design can potentially lead to inaccurate results
  - Examples of subtle alterations (biases) in trials that could influence outcomes in a positive direction:
    - Comparison of drug doses that are likely not close to an equivalent comparison (i.e. omeprazole 10 mg compared versus pantoprazole 40 mg daily)
    - Underrepresentation of a group of individuals unlikely to respond to a targeted therapy (i.e. elderly and chemotherapy)

PHI (Protected Health Information)

- Any information about a patient's health, care provided, or payment that is obtained by a "Covered Entity" (i.e. a healthcare institution or professional)
- If the above information can be linked to an individual patient, it should be considered PHI

Principles of Medication Use Evaluation (MUE)

- Analyzes the entire process of medication use
  - Prescribing
  - Ordering
  - Preparing
  - Dispensing
  - Administering
  - Monitoring
- Useful for
  - Supporting and identifying ideal medication therapy
  - Preventing errors, injuries and adverse reactions (i.e. maximizing safety)
  - Maximizing potential benefits of medication therapy
  - Working together with all disciplines to ensure best practices are done

- o Continuous improvement
- o Enhancing standardization
- o Identifying areas of weakness/education needs
- o Minimizing costs
- o Satisfying regulatory requirements

Formulary

- List of medications approved by a governing body, institution, company, etc. (i.e. hospital, insurance company)
- Updated regularly
- Considerations in selecting the formulary
  - o Guidelines, standards, and best practices
  - o Cost effectiveness

Pharmacy and Therapeutics Committee (P and T)

- In an institution, they are responsible for creating, editing, and managing the formulary
- Composed of a multidisciplinary team
  - o Physicians
  - o Pharmacists
  - o Nurses

- o   Administration
- o   Advanced practice providers (NPs, PAs)
- o   Quality improvement
- o   Other healthcare professionals as deemed appropriate
- Medication use evaluation is an important function of the P&T committee
- Errors, adverse drug reactions, and guidelines are all examples of items the P&T committee might evaluate to assess medications and determine appropriateness of continued use as well as best processes involved in using these medications

Drug Enforcement Agency (DEA)

DEA Objective

- "Enforces" rules/laws on the use of controlled substances
- Seeks to reduce/prevent drug smuggling, drug abuse, and unauthorized use of controlled substances

DEA Schedules 1-5

- Schedule 1: Drugs with no accepted medical use and a high potential for abuse
    - Common examples: methamphetamine, LSD, heroin, marijuana
- Schedule 2: Drugs with accepted medical uses, but a high potential for abuse
    - Common examples: amphetamine salts, fentanyl, oxycodone, hydrocodone, hydromorphone,

morphine, methadone and methylphenidate
- Schedule 3: Drugs with a moderate or low potential for psychological and physical dependence; less abuse risk than drugs that are classified as schedule 1 or 2
    o Common examples: acetaminophen with codeine, dronabinol, testosterone, buprenorphine/naloxone
- Schedule 4: Drugs with a low potential for abuse and a low risk of dependence
    o Common examples: lorazepam, diazepam, tramadol, zolpidem, midazolam, phenobarbital
- Schedule 5: Drugs with lower potential for abuse than schedule 4, and often contain low amounts of narcotics
    o Common examples: Lomotil, pregabalin, Robitussin AC (less than 200 mg/100milliliters)
- ***States may have stricter scheduling, follow the stricter schedule

DEA Number Verification

- Each DEA number has two letters and 7 numbers

- The 1st letter indicates the kind of provider/institution (i.e. physician, pharmacy, manufacturer, etc.)
- The 2nd letter in the DEA number is the 1st letter in the last name of the provider
- Numerical calculation to verify DEA authenticity
    - 1st – Add the 1st, 3rd, and 5th digits
    - 2nd – Add the 2nd, 4th, and 6th digits together and multiply that sum by 2
    - Add the 1st step and 2nd step together
    - The 7th digit of the DEA number should equal the second number in the sum
- Example: Dr. John Evenson
    - BE1324376
    - B indicates that the number belongs to a physician which is accurate in the example
    - E represents the first letter of the prescribers last name which is accurate in the example
    - Add digits 1, 3, 5; 1+2+3 = 6
    - Add digits 2, 4, 6; 3+4+7 = 14 (X2) = 28
    - 6+28 = 34
    - The "4" in 34 does not equal the 7th digit which is a 6
        - This would be a falsified or incorrect DEA number
- Provider's hospital code number

- Providers may utilize a hospital's DEA number
- That DEA number may have additional numbers at the end to indicate which individual prescribed a controlled substance under the hospital's DEA number
- Example: AB1234567-031 (last 3 digits indicate the individual within an institution that prescribed the controlled substance)

Providers Exempt from DEA Registration

- U.S. Army
- Navy
- Marine Corps
- Air Force
- Coast Guard
- Public Health Service
- Bureau of Prisons
- **Must state the type of service they are working in on the prescription for the controlled substance (i.e. U.S. Army)
- **Must also state their service ID number
- **Public Health providers' service ID number is their social security number

Electronic Prescriptions for Controlled Substances

- Computer to computer transmission is acceptable
- Computer to fax is not acceptable
  - Must print, sign, then fax if going to use a fax machine
- Schedule 2's can only be faxed in the following circumstances:
  - Hospice (to be noted on the Rx)
  - LTC/Nursing homes (Home Care, Assisted Living are not acceptable unless the patient living there is enrolled in hospice)
  - Home infusion
- Note, when this is allowed the faxed Rx is the original and should be filed accordingly
- A physician may fax a schedule 2 Rx for patient convenience (ensure that the prescription is ready quickly) as long as the original is brought in and given to the pharmacist prior to dispensing
  - Pharmacist must verify that the scripts, faxed and hard copy, match
  - Use paper copy that was brought in as the original
- DEA must approve of the program that is being used to send the electronic prescription

- Physician should NOT print a backup copy and give to patient if the electronic transmission went through (printing for in clinic record keeping is ok)
- In the event of unsuccessful E-prescription transmission, a physician should note that there was an attempt to E-prescribe the medication on the prescription and that the transmission failed
  - Time, date and pharmacy must be noted – which makes sense because the patient could take the hard copy to another pharmacy
  - Pharmacy that receives the hard copy with this warning must do their due diligence to ensure that the electronic submission failed and the prescription was never filled

Electronic Prescriptions – Schedule 2 Controlled Substances

- Allowed under federal law/DEA
- Two-factor credential is acceptable for authorization of controlled substances (i.e. a password and a fingerprint reader)
- Some states may still have restrictions
- Requirements for information on prescription similar to written prescription

- Allowable to do multiple prescriptions up to the 90-day period

Electronic Records

- DEA allows electronic records
- Electronic records must be able to capture and retain the following information:
  - Rx #
  - Date Rx was written
  - Refill dates
  - Name and address of the patient
  - Name, address, and DEA # of prescriber
  - Drug, strength, dosage form, and quantity (dispensed and remaining)
  - Refills remaining on the prescription
  - Pharmacist who dispensed each refill (initials or other way of identification)
- Length of record keeping for DEA is a minimum of 2 years (review state law which may be longer than this)

Requirements for a Prescription

- Name, address, practitioner's full name, DEA registration number
- Drug name

- Dosage form and strength
- Quantity
- Direction
- Refills (if appropriate)

Who May Prescribe a Controlled Substance

- Physician
- Dentist
- Specialists (within scope of practice)
- Veterinarian
- Mid-level provider (nurse practitioner, physician assistant)
- Must be licensed within the state or jurisdiction that they practice
- Must be registered with the DEA
- An employee of an institution working within their usual practice, in place of their own registration, with specific requirements needing to be met
- Prescriptions for research purposes are NOT allowed
- A prescription for a controlled substance supply delivered to a provider for purposes of dispensing to patients is NOT allowed

Schedule 2 Controlled Substances – What can be changed on the Rx?

- DEA has minimal guidance
- Refers pharmacist to use professional judgement and follow state and federal laws
- Review state law with regards to what can be changed
- DEA requirements for a C2 prescription
  - Date
  - Provider name, address, and signature
  - Name and address of the patient
  - Drug, dose, dosage form
  - Quantity
  - Directions
  - DEA #

Schedule 2 Controlled Substances – Multiple Prescriptions

- 90 days is ok (i.e. 3 prescriptions of 30 days is allowed to be issued at a time) – see state laws as some may be more strict
- Usual DEA rules apply, such as, legitimate condition, scope of practice, etc.
- Provider must feel as if there is low risk of diversion

- Each Rx must be written on a separate prescription (electronic is acceptable)
- Instructions must be given as to the date when the future prescription(s) can be filled

Who Owns the Prescription?

- The patient has a right to their own prescription as long as the prescription has not been filled and dispensed to the patient
- Once filled and dispensed, it is the legal property of the pharmacy
- A copy can be given to patients so long as the pharmacist notes that it is a copy and has been filled already to prevent the patient from illegally trying to fill it elsewhere

Schedule 2 Controlled Substances – Partial Filling

- There are a few reasons why it may be necessary or appropriate to consider partial filling a schedule 2 controlled substance, a few examples include:
  - Pharmacy does not have enough medication to fill the entire prescription

- o Terminally ill or LTC patient (must be verified and documented on the prescription)
- Low Inventory
  - o Pharmacist should note the amount that was dispensed
  - o Must fill the remaining within 72 hours
    - If not filled within 72 hours, new Rx is required
- LTC/Terminally ill
  - o Partial dispensing is allowable
  - o 60-day window to give partial fills
    - Once 60 days is up from original Rx date, you may not dispense any more medication under that prescription
- Partial fill must take place at same pharmacy and location (cannot finish partial fill at a different Walgreens, Walmart, CVS, etc. location)
- With each partial fill, the following should be documented
  - o Date of partial fill
  - o Amount dispensed
  - o Drug quantity that is left for the Rx
  - o Signature or initials of pharmacist providing the partial fill

Schedule 2 Controlled Substances – Emergency Filling

- Telephone emergency Rx is allowed
- Quantity should only be for the emergency time period; the emergency period can be no greater than 72 hours
- A written Rx should be provided to the dispensing pharmacy
- Written Rx should be postmarked or received within 7 days of the emergency prescription
- Pharmacy should contact local DEA office if the prescription has not been received after the 7-day period
- File away written Rx right with the telephone prescription that was taken for the emergency period
- Make a note on the prescription that indicates that it was "authorized for emergency dispensing"
- It is allowed to receive an E-script as the "written copy" as long as the sending facility/provider is authorized to provide electronic controlled substance prescriptions

Schedule 3-5 Controlled Substances

- Refills are allowed

- For schedule 3 and 4, refills are good for 6 months or up to a maximum of 5 times (from the date that the prescription was written, NOT from the date of the first fill)
  - Under federal law, schedule 5 does not have the same requirements as schedule 3 and 4 - review state laws as many do include schedule 5 to have only a 6-month expiration
  - Federal law allows refilling of schedule 5 medication to be up to the practitioner
- Faxes are acceptable under federal law
- Telephone prescriptions are acceptable under federal law
- E-prescriptions and written signed prescriptions are probably the most common

Schedule 3-5 Controlled Substances Recordkeeping

- Drug, dosage form
- Fill and refill dates
- Amount dispensed
- Refills remaining
- Initials of pharmacist who fills/refills

Schedule 3-5 Controlled Substances – Partial Filling

- Ok to do partial fills
- Rx is good for a maximum of 6 months
- If Rx says "3" refills, you may do more than that in partial fills as long as the total quantity on the prescription is not exceeded

Transfer of a Controlled Substance

- Schedule 2 controlled substance is not allowed to be transferred to another pharmacy
- Transfer of a Schedule 3-5 is allowed on a one-time basis per DEA rules

Labeling "Caution" for Controlled Substances

- All controlled substance prescriptions dispensed to patients must contain a notification on the label that states: "Caution: Federal law prohibits the transfer of this drug to any person other than the patient for whom it was prescribed."

- One exception includes research purposes where participants are to be blinded in the clinical investigation

Electronic Prescriptions and Two-Factor Authentication

- DEA requires two-factor authentication for prescribing controlled substances
- Two-factor authentication meets legal requirements and is considered the same as a physical signature
- Two-factor authentication entails two of the following three principles:
  - A physical object (a fob key that only the prescriber can access)
  - A password or something that is known by the prescriber
  - Something that can physically identify the prescriber (fingerprint, retina scan)

Drugs for Addiction/Dependence

- Drugs with buprenorphine (Buprenes, Belbuca, Subutex, Suboxone, etc.) – schedule 3 controlled substance
- Buprenorphine
  - X-waiver requirement eliminated (only certain prescribers with specific training could prescribe this medication)
  - Prescribing buprenorphine for opioid use disorder simply requires a standard DEA registration
  - Limit removed on the number of patients that one prescriber may treat for opioid use disorder using buprenorphine
  - ***States may still have stricter requirements
- Consolidated Appropriations Act of 2023 – prescribers need to have at least 1 of the following to prescribe buprenorphine
  - 8 hours of training on opioid/substance abuse disorders
  - Board certification in addiction medicine or addiction psychiatry
  - Graduated with a PA, NP, or medical degree within 5 years and received educational curriculum of at least 8

hours surrounding opioid or other
substance use disorders
- Buprenorphine for pain or other indications
may be filled if deemed clinically appropriate
by the pharmacist

Methadone for Addiction

- Methadone Rx for pain may be filled without
any special registration
- If methadone is for the treatment of
addiction, it may only be used by a narcotic
treatment facility; this requires that the
facility be registered with the DEA to provide
these services
  - During the COVID Public Health
Emergency, exceptions were made to
allow for at home methadone for 28
or 14 days depending upon
documented patient stability
- Most normal pharmacies will NOT be able to
dispense methadone for addiction purposes

Performing a Controlled Substance Inventory

- Federal law – at a minimum, inventory should be performed on an every other year basis
- If inventory is done January 31st 2019, it would need to be done again by or on January 30th 2021
- Documentation necessary with inventory:
    - Time and date of when the inventory was taken
    - Drug, dose, and dosage form
    - Quantity on hand
- C3-C5 controlled substances can be estimated as long as package size is 1,000 or less
    - Exact count is necessary if container is over 1,000 tablets, capsules, etc.
- C2s
    - Exact count is necessary
- In the event a drug becomes a scheduled substance, the day it becomes scheduled, an inventory must be done (tramadol, for example, was changed a few years ago from a traditional prescription medication to a controlled substance)

DEA Forms

- Form 41
    - Used for destruction of controlled substances
    - These controlled substances should be under the possession of the pharmacy (NOT previously dispensed and returned by customers)
    - Important drug documentation requirements
        - Drug, dosage form
        - Quantity
        - Name, phone, and address of pharmacy
        - Signature of destroyer and witness's signature
        - Method of destruction
    - Can be done on an annual basis
    - Witnessed by at least two people who shall be a pharmacist, physician, mid-level practitioner, nurse, or law enforcement

- Form 106
    - Loss or theft of controlled substances
    - Language is vague in that the pharmacy should report "significant losses"
    - No definition on what is considered a significant loss

- 1 tablet is probably not considered significant unless there is a major trend; losing 1 tablet every day of the same drug for a month would likely be considered significant
- 1 bottle of 100 would likely be considered significant loss
  - Items to consider to determine if there is significant loss:
    - Amount of drug missing
    - Patterns for a specific drug
    - Other patterns that seem suspicious
  - Information necessary on form 106
    - Name, address and phone number of the location where the controlled substances were lost or stolen
    - DEA registration number
    - Date(s) of loss/theft
    - Patterns of loss in the previous 2 years
    - Type of loss - theft during hours of operation, employee, customer, transmission in route from the manufacturer
    - Action taken to resolve, prevent, or identify the problem
    - Drug, dose, amount, and NDC

- If theft or significant loss of controlled substances is known, the DEA should be made aware by phone or fax immediately, as well as police if dictated by state law
  - 106 should be filled out in addition
- The supplier is responsible for reporting if the pharmacy has never signed in an order and received shipment
- Once the pharmacist has signed in an order and notes a significant loss or theft, then the pharmacy/pharmacist would be responsible for reporting

- Form 222
  - Form used for ordering or transferring schedule 2 controlled substances
  - Electronic ordering/transferring acceptable as long as the program/process has been approved by the DEA
  - Electronic order is called the CSOS (Controlled Substance Ordering System)
  - Paper form has three different colored carbon copies
    - Brown – goes to the supplier of the drug(s)
    - Green – goes to the DEA

- - Blue – stays with the purchaser or recipient of the drug(s)
    - There are only 10 lines on the DEA form, so if more drugs are needed you must use an additional form
  - Information to be documented on the 222 form include:
    - Transaction date
    - Drug, strength, dosage form, quantity
    - Name of drug supplier and address
  - Each pharmacist that the pharmacy wants to allow access to order must have a power of attorney order in place to be able to authorize an order
  - Transfer from pharmacy to pharmacy is acceptable as long as it is under 5% of the controlled substance usage (amount dispensed) for a 1 year period
    - If above this amount, the pharmacy will have to get a wholesaler permit
- Form 224
  - Pharmacy registration that is required by the DEA if controlled drugs are to be dispensed from that pharmacy
  - 224a – Pharmacy renewal

- 224b – Intended for pharmacies that operate a chain of pharmacies

- Form 363
  - Narcotic treatment program registration

Prescription Drug Monitoring Programs (PDMPs)

- A program that allows the pharmacist, prescriber, DEA, and other authorized individuals to monitor and collect information to help ensure that controlled substances are not being excessively prescribed to and received by patients
- Essentially, an electronically accessible database for healthcare professionals to help identify drug diversion
- The majority of states have PDMPs available
- Allows for review of controlled substance prescriptions dispensed to the patient so the health care professional can adequately determine if the current prescription is appropriate to be dispensed
- Helps prevent drug diversion and ensure that legitimate prescriptions are dispensed appropriately

- States may vary in which drugs are monitored (i.e. C2-4 vs. C2-5)
- Some states may require that the PDMP be accessed prior to prescribing or dispensing of a controlled substance
- States have varying requirements on how often the prescription data needs to be reported to the PDMP (real-time, end of the day, etc.)
- Many states are now interconnected so data can be reviewed from multiple states – especially important for states that may share a border where access to pharmacies in another state may be very easy

Pseudoephedrine Regulations

- Limits placed on amount of pseudoephedrine that can be purchased
- No more than 3.6 grams can be purchased in one day
- 9-gram max in 30 days (mail-order is less at 7.5 grams per 30-day period)
- Needs to be locked up or behind the pharmacy counter
- Sales must be noted with the following information
  - Signature
  - Address

o   Date/time of purchase
  o   Visual ID check

Marijuana - Schedule 1 Controlled Substance

- Defined as a drug with a high potential for abuse without an accepted medical indication; lack of safety
- Many states have now reclassified marijuana into a different category
- Many medical facilities that accept Medicare (hospitals, long term care, etc.) and other federal funds still have concerns with allowing non-FDA approved marijuana based products within their facility as it still remains on the schedule 1 controlled substance list
- The enforcement of marijuana by the DEA can depend upon the current administration's desire to enforce the laws
- Facilities (i.e. hospitals, long term care facilities) are generally leery about having policies accepting the use of medical marijuana as they accept money from federal agencies like Medicare and Medicaid

Compounding and Manufacturing

Compounding Medications

- Compounded drugs that have never gone through the FDAs three phases of approval may be used under certain circumstances
- They should be made for a specific patient pursuant to a prescription from a provider
- Anticipatory compounding is allowed (compounding with expectation for a prescription due to routine, refills, or prescribing trends)
- Good manufacturing processes which are applicable to manufacturers are not applicable to compounded drugs
  - This doesn't mean that there are not standards (see USP standards below)
- If drug product is commercially available, it should not be compounded; the exception might be drug shortage

USP – United States Pharmacopeia

- Non-profit organization
- Published with a list of drugs in the National Formulary (USP-NF)
- Sets standard for drugs - all prescription and OTC drugs must meet USP-NF standards
- Laws are set based off of these standards
- USP does NOT do law enforcement (FDA etc. uses USP standards and actually enforces laws/rules)
- "Adulterated" drugs don't meet USP standards for strength, quality or purity

USP 795

- Chapter in USP that develops standards on non-sterile compounding (often done in community/retail pharmacy)
- Goal of USP is to minimize risks like infection, contamination, and erroneous dosing
- Beyond-use dating guidance contained within the chapter
- Nonsterile compounding is preparing, mixing, or creating a drug product based upon a provider's prescription
- This product should not be commercially available and should be made for a specific

patient (do not do batch compounding as this could be considered manufacturing)

- Compounding medications increases risk for errors and contamination, so the commercially manufactured product is considered safer and superior
- Pharmacies can do non-sterile compounding under 503A, for compounded products for a specific patient (FDA guidance)
- Pharmacies cannot "bulk" compound unless registered under section 503B
    - Pharmacy may "anticipate" orders based on routine (i.e. child is on chronic therapy for seizures)
- 3 categories of nonsterile compounding;
    - Simple - making a preparation that has a USP compounding monograph, like reconstitution of an amoxicillin suspension, where there is a manufacturer recommendation with spelled out beyond use date and stability data
    - Moderate - compounding that involves calculations or procedures, like mixing of two creams, or making a preparation where stability data is uncertain
    - Complex - any compounding that involves special training, facilities, equipment or procedures (gray area of legality in a community pharmacy

and most will not be compounding these types of medications); creating a transdermal dosage form would be an example

- Ingredients should be of high quality, easily identifiable and purchased from a reliable company

Personnel Requirements for 795

- Staff should demonstrate competency
- Pharmacy should have standardized policies and procedures which may include, but not be limited to;
  - Training
  - Scope
  - Facility/equipment requirements:
    - Potable water (drinking water)
    - Designated area for compounding
    - Cleanliness
    - Plumbing
    - Appropriate containers for disposal
    - Lighting
    - Adequate heat/cooling capabilities
  - Cleaning facilities
  - Formula records
  - Recalls

- Patient reported complaints
- Pharmacist in charge or designated go-to expert
- Board of pharmacy rules and regulations
- Storage
- Cleaning
- Documentation procedures

USP 795 – Beyond Use Dates (BUD)

- Nonaqueous compounds - 6 months or the earliest expiration date of any ingredient (whichever comes first)
- Water containing oral compounds and stored under refrigerated conditions - 14-day max or earliest expiration date, whichever comes first. ANY water in any component or the addition of water will fall into this category
- Water containing topical and semisolid compounds
  - 30 days or earliest expiration, whichever is sooner

USP 797

- Best practices, procedures, guidelines and compliance requirements for STERILE compounding
- USP 797 goals:
  - Ensure quality sterile products
  - Free from contaminants
  - Ensure accuracy and consistency in drug preparation, strength and identity
- Guidelines on clean room:
  - Applies to any institution that is compounding, storing, or dispensing sterile products

Microbial Risk Levels per USP 797

- Low risk situations:
  - Compounding with aseptic technique with ISO (International Organization for Standardization) class 5 or better unit
    - ISO class 5 cleanroom (IV hood) - max of 3,520 particles equal to or larger than 0.5 microns per cubic meter of air
  - Only sterile products and ingredients are used

- Example: using sterile needles/syringes to transfer sterile medication from manufacturer's packaged products
- Mixing 3 or less sterile products
- Storage - 48 hours at room temperature, 14 days when refrigerated, 45 days frozen
- Medium Risk:
  - Putting together multiple doses of sterile products (4 or more)
  - If compounding takes a long time - special dissolution
  - Typically, these mixtures do not have bacteriostatic substances
  - May be administered over days
  - Storage 30 hours at room temperature, 9 days when refrigerated and 45 days frozen
  - TPN is the classic example of a medium risk sterile compound
  - Filling of infusion devices that are administered over several days
  - Most inpatient pharmacies do medium risk on a regular basis
- High Risk:
  - The most common high-risk situation is the use of non-sterile drugs or devices to make a sterile product

- Using anything less than an ISO Class 5 environment will classify this situation as high risk
- Storage - max 24 hours at room temperature, 3 days refrigerated and 45 days frozen
- Example - using non-sterile bulk drug to make a solution; or using non-sterile devices

Personnel and Training USP 797

- Personnel must be adequately trained; initial and ongoing training requirements include:
  - Written testing
  - Routine review/training
  - Facilities should have policies and procedures in place for testing/training staff
  - Media fill test (or aseptic manipulations skills) - this is a test done to prove that no contamination has taken place during the drug preparation phase
    - Annually for low-medium risk manipulations
    - 2 times each year for high risk compounding

Clean Room, Environment and Hood USP 797

- Low and medium risk
  - Air classification must meet ISO class 8 standards
  - ISO class 5 cleanroom
  - Positive pressure system (air flows out of system - used for non-hazardous drugs)
  - Smooth walls, floors, ceilings, and fixtures, no cracks or use of materials that break down
  - Materials should not break down from cleaning agents
  - HEPA Filter removes 99.97% of all particles 0.3 microns or larger
  - Laminar Flow hood - standard hood where air blows toward person; turn on at least 30 minutes prior to compounding to reestablish airflow, generally it is left on, clean if shut off
  - Chemo hood - vertical air flow (you wouldn't want to blow hazardous substances at the compounder); should be left to run continuously
  - Don't place items in front of each other as it disrupts the airflow
  - Gowning
    - No lab coats, make-up, jewelry

- Wash hands to the elbows
- Hair and shoe covers
- Coveralls and coats that fit appropriately (these can be reused for the shift) - hair, shoe covers, etc. should not be reused
- Gloves and face masks are put on in the clean room
    - Only what is necessary should be in hood - no pens, paper, etc.
    - Adjacent area should not have a sink or floor drain (could harbor contaminants) - sometimes referred to anteroom or buffer zone
        - Materials, labels, and gowning equipment are gathered here prior to entering into the clean room
- High risk - only differentiation is that ante area should be a room

797 Requirements

- Need a spelled out quality assurance (QA) program
    - Assesses the entire process of drug prep → dispensing
    - Outlines monitoring and evaluation of processes

- o QA program should state how monitoring results are reported, tracked, and evaluated
- o Spells out what follow-up measures shall be done for systems that are out of the norm
- o Designates a leader or individual responsible for each task/monitoring parameter
- Cleaning
  - o Process spelled out in procedures/policies
  - o At minimum, should be done at beginning of each shift (per USP)
  - o Cleanest to dirtiest
    - ▪ Ceiling →back →sides →bar, devices → main surface
    - ▪ Go from back to front, do not touch the HEPA filter
    - ▪ Use isopropyl alcohol 70%

USP 800 – Hazardous Drugs

- Defines best practices for protecting healthcare workers from exposure to hazardous drugs as well as promote patient safety and environmental protection
- Must be stored and prepared to prevent exposure to healthcare workers

- Important regulatory agencies that protect workers
  - OSHA - Occupational Safety and Health Administration, sets and enforces standards to protect healthcare workers
  - NIOSH (National Institute for Occupational Safety and Health - conducts research and makes recommendations on whether drugs are classified as hazardous or not
- Drug has at least one of the following six characteristics to be considered hazardous:
  - Carcinogenic
  - Teratogenic
  - Reproductive toxicity
  - Organ toxicity at low doses
  - Genotoxicity
  - Novel agents that have similar structures and/or toxicity to a currently classified hazardous drug
- Personal Protective Equipment (PPE)
  - For administration of all chemo hazardous drugs, two pairs of chemo tested gloves must be worn
  - For administration of injectable hazardous drugs (HDs), chemo resistant gowns must be worn in addition to the chemo gloves

- For compounding, all equipment must be removed when leaving the compounding area
- Cannot reuse gowns after leaving the compounding area
- Must have separate equipment for compounding hazardous drugs versus non-hazardous drugs

Manufacturing

- Producing large quantities of drugs that are massed produce for resale
- Manufacturers must comply with FDA requirements and regulations
- Pharmacies should not be manufacturing unless they have an authorized license and registration from the FDA to do so

Manufacturing Expiration Dating

- Expiration date will only have a month and year on a manufacturer label
  - I.e. 11/2027
- The last day of the month would be the expiration date

- In our example above of November 2027, the expiration date would be November 30th, 2027

Good Manufacturing Processes (GMP)

- Rules and regulations regarding the production of pharmaceuticals
- Focuses on practices that ensure quality, accuracy, and safety of pharmaceuticals
- Rules will apply to any agency, individuals, or company that is mass producing pharmaceuticals
- Facilities are audited by the FDA approximately every other year

---

New England Compounding Pharmacy

- Meningitis outbreak
- Patient got sick due to drugs not being produced according to good manufacturing process

- Injectable drugs were being manufactured for use by healthcare organizations across the country
- The New England Compounding Center was classified as a compounding pharmacy only, not a manufacturer, so the FDA had minimal oversight
  - State board of pharmacy was the agency with oversight about what they were doing
- Drug Quality and Security Act was enacted by Congress in 2013
  - This gave the FDA more authority and power to oversee and create regulations differentiating compounding and manufacturing
  - FDA 503A compounding pharmacy can only create drugs pursuant to a prescription for a specific patient; this type of pharmacy cannot make drugs for bulk use in a clinic office type setting
    - This has created more challenges for clinics and offices to obtain medications for bulk use
  - FDA 503B compounding pharmacy can do bulk compounding
  - May sell larger quantities to healthcare institutions for office use as patients need them
  - 503B pharmacies have higher level requirements for monitoring, tracking,

and reporting than a 503A pharmacy; additionally, all the requirements for good manufacturing processes need to be followed

Unit Dose Labeling Requirements

- Hospitals often desire to repackage pharmaceuticals into unit dose formulations to allow for easier administration
- Repackaging tablets into an individual dose is often done
- The following label requirements must be met:
  - Name of drug and amount contained within the individual dosing unit
  - Lot and expiration date
  - Identification as to the manufacturer or distributor
  - Additional information as applicable for the drug (i.e. exposure warnings, refrigeration requirements, etc.)

Repackaging Unit Dose & Beyond Use Dating

- FDA suggests a maximum beyond use date of 6 months or 25% of the time remaining on the manufacturer bottle expiration date (whichever is less)
- If there are studies available, the expiration date can be extended according to that literature

Are you finding this review helpful? If so, I'd love a kind rating/review on Amazon! If questions or comments, email me @ mededucation101@gmail.com**, thanks!**

Labeling, Naming, Pharmacist, and Technician Requirements

Over-the-Counter Labeling Requirements

- Name of product
- Indication
- Manufacturer
- Amount
- Patient instructions and warnings (i.e. pregnancy, adverse effects, etc.)
- Active and Inactive ingredients
- FDA phone # and "Questions?" statement
- Other information that may be relevant (i.e. storage, packaging information, etc.)
- Tamper-evident seal to ensure that the product is not used if that seal is broken

Labeling of Prescription Products – Requirements

- Brand (if applicable) and generic name
- Dose
- Amount contained within the package
  - May be in weight, number, or volume depending upon the type of dosage form
- Dosage form type
- Manufacturer and location
- For Rx only statement; "Caution: Federal law prohibits dispensing without a prescription"
- Package insert and reference to that insert for more information
- NDC information
- Lot number
- If controlled drug, it needs an indicator of what schedule the drug is
- Storage information
- Expiration date

National Drug Code (NDC)

- Each drug or medical type product will have a National Drug Code (NDC) number

- NDC is a 10-digit FDA assigned number that is unique to each individual product
- Example number: 8294-2837-01
  - The first four digits (8294) is given to a company by the FDA to identify their products, this is called the "labeler" code (I.e. which company makes the product)
  - The middle four digits are called the product code which identifies the drug product (i.e. 50 mg of tramadol)
  - The final 2 digits are indicative of what type of packaging the drug or product is contained within (i.e. 100 tablet bottle versus 1,000 tablet bottle)
- NDC codes are often used in documentation to identify which product was given
  - This can be helpful for billing purposes and in any type of recall where a patient may have received a product that was later found to be harmful (or potentially harmful) in some way

Naming of Drugs

- Chemical name
  - Describes the drugs chemical structure
  - Often very large and not practical for use in practice

- o May be given a shorthand name (compound K-675) during research for ease of discussion and writing into research literature
- Generic name
  - o Considered the official name of a drug
  - o Once a drug is approved by the FDA, the drug will receive a generic name, as well as a brand name
  - o Name is assigned by the FDA
- Brand name
  - o Company requests this name and the FDA approves it
  - o FDA may reject if it sounds too much like the generic name or another brand name – this could cause significant confusion and may increase the risk of medical errors

Adulteration

- Adulteration is defined as a drug that does not meet FDA standards in one of the following:
  - o Quality
  - o Strength
  - o Purity
- Examples of adulterated drugs:
  - o Drugs that were damaged in a flood or fire

- o Drugs that are moldy or dirty due to inappropriate storage

Misbranding

- Misbranding is defined by erroneous, inadequate or misleading labeling
- Examples of misbranded drugs:
    - o Receiving a bottle of generic sildenafil without a noted strength on the label
    - o Receiving enalapril pills in a bottle that is labeled lisinopril
    - o An OTC drug that does not follow FDA requirements for labeling
- It is possible for a product to be both misbranded and adulterated

Inactive and Active Ingredients

- Inactive ingredients are any part of a drug product that is not the active ingredient(s)
- Required by law for manufacturers to identify what inactive ingredients go into their drug formulation
- Active ingredient is the part(s) of a drug product that is intended to have a physiological action or pharmacological activity on the body; it is the substance(s) of

the drug product that is intended to cure,
treat, manage, prevent, or diagnosis a disease

Package Insert Requirements

- Description of the drug - chemical structure,
  classification, and makeup of the drug with
  both the active and inactive ingredients
- Clinical pharmacology which describes the
  best-known information about how the drug
  works in the body to provide its clinical
  benefit
- Indications and usage describes what the
  drug is used for and what indications have
  been approved by the FDA
- Dosage and administration information
- Boxed warnings if applicable
- Contraindications – any situations where a
  patient should not take this medication
- Warnings – situations where caution should
  be used; this could be in a particular disease
  state, at a certain dose, recognition of
  problems with abrupt cessation/reduction, or
  in situations where a drug interaction may be
  problematic
- Adverse reactions
- Drug interactions
- Pregnancy, breastfeeding considerations or
  considerations in other populations like

pediatrics or geriatrics and whether or not the drug is safe to use

- Carcinogenesis risk
- Precautions – situations where the drug may pose a higher risk to certain patients
- Information for patients – important education points patients should be aware of when using the medication
- Laboratory tests that may be required or recommended with use of the drug
- Overdose information
- How the drug is supplied
- References and clinical studies that are applicable to the drug and FDA approval

Pregnancy, Lactation and Reproductive Requirements

- Eliminated the historic category system of A-X when it comes to pregnancy and medications
- The Pregnancy and Lactation Labeling Rule (PLLR) was created by the FDA to replace the pregnancy categories
- The ambiguous information associated with the A-X categories prompted the FDA to act and change what is required on the drug labeling

- The labeling now must include information for use in specific populations
  - Pregnancy, including labor and delivery
  - Lactation
  - Possible reproductive issues for males and females

Pharmacist-In-Charge (PIC)

- State law will dictate responsibilities
- At a minimum, PIC will likely be responsible for the following:
  - Following federal and state requirements (laws and rules)
    - DEA
    - OSHA
    - Labor laws
    - Pharmacy practice laws
    - FDA
  - Work environment and physical space
    - Lighting
    - Counseling space
    - Individual work space areas
    - Compounding equipment requirements
    - Cleaning stations (i.e. sink with hot and cold water, eye wash station), compounding areas, and other designated areas

- Security
  - Ensuring licensing and training of staff
  - Ensure appropriate licensing and permits for the pharmacy
  - Ensuring appropriate breaks and working conditions
  - Safety of staff (OSHA requirements)
  - Access to the pharmacy
  - Reference books/online resources
  - Written policies and procedures
  - Drug inventory requirements
  - Supervision of staff

Refusal to Fill a Prescription

- Pharmacists may refuse to fill a medication but must have a legitimate reason
- Reasons may include:
  - Illegal or illegitimate prescription
  - Does not have a product or cannot order the product
  - In the pharmacist's clinical judgement, there is significant safety risk to the patient

Common Pharmacy Technician Responsibilities

- ***All responsibilities shall be done under the supervision of the pharmacist
- Aiding in the dispensing of medications
  - Labeling
  - Counting
  - Insurance billing
- Aiding in compounding drugs
- Ordering drugs
- Stocking drugs
- Data collection
- Contacting and speaking with customers about non-clinical issues
- Communication with physicians' offices about non-clinical concerns
- Cashier activities
- ***Check state laws as certain activities, particularly in the setting of transfers and accepting orders may be allowed if technicians have met certain standards for certification

Common Activities Technicians Are Not Qualified For

- Clinical review of medications
- Drug utilization review
- Discussion with prescriber regarding the use of a medication
- Rx transfers
- Receiving verbal orders for prescriptions or prescription changes
- Clinical discussions with patients
- Patient counseling

Tech-check-tech (TCT)

- A more recent development that some states have undertaken
- Pharmacy technicians check the filling of other technicians to ensure that the correct product was dispensed to the patient
- Essentially, pharmacy technicians are doing the final check of the physical product that is going to the patient
- More likely to occur in the inpatient setting where automated dispensing machines are utilized

- States that have used TCT often have additional requirements and/or certifications that the technician must complete

Pharmacist to Pharmacy Technician Ratios

- Set by each individual state, check state law

Pharmacist Counselling

- OBRA - Omnibus Budget Reconciliation Act of 1990 (federal legislation)
- OBRA required that Medicaid patients have an improved understanding of their medications
- Many states were forced to alter their own rules on what is the expectation for the pharmacist
- Important OBRA provisions included:
  - Clinical review prior to dispensing (Prospective DUR)
    - Drug-drug, drug-disease interactions
    - Allergies
    - Over/under use of the medication

- - Dose appropriateness
  - Duplicate therapy
  - Counseling requirements
    - Name, dose, route, frequency of administration
    - How to administer the medication
    - Indication and expected results
    - Drug-drug, drug-food interactions
    - Side effects
    - Refill information
    - Missed dose education
    - Storage
    - Refill information
  - Record keeping
    - Name, address, phone #, DOB
    - Gender
    - Drug list
    - Pharmacist notes about the patient
    - Allergies, conditions, and ADRs
  - Retrospective drug review – left up to states to determine what is required

Drug Samples

- Legislation was created in the Prescription Drug Marketing Act (PDMA) that created stipulations for the use and promotion of samples by manufacturers, pharmacies, and other healthcare institutions

- Drug manufacturers are required to document and maintain records of the drug and the quantity that are given away
- May only be distributed to those who write a formal request
- Most often requested by individual practitioners, who must be licensed in the state that they are making the request from
- Name, address, and signature of the requesting individual should also be documented by the pharmaceutical company giving out the samples
- Electronic submission to the FDA is encouraged

Compounding Documentation

- Can vary based upon state rules and regulations
- Commonly documented components of non-sterile compounding:
  - Name, strength, and dosage form of final compounded product and products that are used to create the formulation (lot #, expiration date, manufacturer for each product used)
  - Quantity compounded

- Calculations necessary to determine appropriate formula for compounded product; many pharmacies will have a master list of compounded products so that calculations do not need to be done every time a product is compounded
- Stability and compatibility references as applicable
- Compounding instructions as applicable, such as, mixing order, temperature necessary for melting, etc.
- Documentation of any quality issues; patient reported issues or possible errors in the preparation
- Labeling information is similar to regular prescription labeling with a few exceptions:
  - Beyond use date
  - Appropriate storage as applicable
  - Final product description
  - Control # or Rx#
  - Date of preparation

Prescribing Practices

Self-Prescribing

- No federal law prohibiting self-prescribing
- Medical code of ethics discourages self-prescribing
- Review state laws - individual states may have laws against it
  - Especially controlled substances
  - Also, it is generally discouraged to prescribe for immediate family members as well

Off-Label Uses

- Using a drug for a condition that is not approved in the formal labeling from the FDA
  - In addition, using a different dose or alternative route of administration that has not been approved would be considered off-label as well
- Very frequently done in practice

- Allowable under law within the scope of practice of the prescribing provider and if the drug is deemed medically appropriate
- Reasons for off-label use:
  o FDA approved drug to treat the condition doesn't exist
  o All FDA approved drugs have been tried and stopped due to ineffectiveness or intolerability
- Manufacturers may not advertise off-label uses without an FDA approved indication
- Manufacturers MAY distribute peer-reviewed literature on off-label uses

Retired, Deceased, or Suspended Providers

- Questions may arise about whether a prescription can be filled if a provider has changed their status as a licensed provider
- Need to refer to state laws
- Answer is likely, "no" as these prescriptions cannot be filled with most states
- Many will reference that a therapeutic relationship is necessary between a patient and provider for drug therapy to be valid; this isn't possible with non-practicing providers

Foreign Providers and Out of State Provider Prescriptions

- Dictated by state laws and who is authorized to practice medicine within that state
  - Review state laws/rules on this topic
- Many states will allow out of state prescriptions to be filled as long as the pharmacist feels that it is clinically appropriate and legitimate
- Foreign providers may be more restricted by states

Mailing Prescriptions

- Mailing or accepting a mailed prescription is perfectly legal
- Physician offices mailing a written prescription to a patient and them bring the prescription to a pharmacy is also legal
- It is obviously illegal for anyone to open the mailed prescription without authorization and get the medication filled; both the act of stealing mail and attempting to falsely fill a prescription not intended for the end user
- Controlled substance prescriptions by a foreign provider are not allowed by the Drug Enforcement Agency (DEA)

Collaborative Practice Agreement

- A collaborative practice agreement (CPA) is a formal arrangement between a licensed provider (or a group of providers) and a registered pharmacist (or group of pharmacists). The agreement allows a pharmacist to perform specific delegated patient care functions. In general, most of the functions involve changing medications or altering medication dosing. Examples include, but are not limited to, antibiotic dosing, warfarin dosing, diabetes management, hypertension management, or hyperlipidemia management.
- The scope and ability to collaborate with other healthcare professionals are typically defined by state laws

Did you find this review helpful? If so, I'd love a rating and review on Amazon! Thanks in advance! – Eric Christianson, PharmD

State Pharmacy Law Questions – Self-Study

MPJE Study Questions	Answer
Technician ratio – hospital?	
Technician ratio – community/retail?	
Technician training requirements?	
Tech-check-tech program allowed by state? If so, requirements?	

Is a prescription from retired, dead, suspended license practitioner allowable? Under which circumstances, if any?	
How long to keep prescription records? (DEA is typically 2 years)	
Who is allowed to transfer prescription records?	
Mailing narcotics/controlled substance rules?	
Sudafed (pseudoephedrine) rules if different from federal?	
Stricter schedule for a controlled drug? Which one(s)? (i.e. tramadol, gabapentin, etc.)	
Who is allowed to give immunizations? What training is necessary?	

Notification of disaster to board of pharmacy (flood, tornado, hurricane, etc.) – what timeframe?	
Technician education/certification requirements?	
Intern requirements? When can they apply to be an intern? How many hours? Type of hours necessary?	
Filling scripts from out of state providers or foreign providers?	
Restrictions on prescription transfers?	
Day supply rules/laws?	
Medical marijuana laws/rules?	

Continuing education requirements?	
Preceptor registration and requirements?	
Over-the-counter needles purchase? Allowed? How many?	
Length of time that prescription is valid for?	
Take back and repository programs?	
Collaborative practice rules and regulations?	
References required within a pharmacy?	
Required equipment?	

Space requirements for workers/compounding?	
Documentation necessary for refusal of counseling?	
Mandatory work breaks or unique worker's rights?	
Rules on returning drugs to the pharmacy?	
License fees, how often do you need to renew?	
License posting rules?	
Requirements for closing a pharmacy or changing ownership?	

Reciprocity requirements?	
Pharmacist in-charge (PIC) responsibilities?	
Can practitioners dispense? What restrictions if any, do they have?	
Pharmacists right to refuse a prescription (Plan B, abortion, etc.)?	
Requirements to report vaccine administration?	
Requirements for reporting dispensed medications and accessing the prescription drug monitoring program database? Who can access the data and how can they share it?	

State sponsored addiction programs available for healthcare professionals?	
Rules regarding pharmacists dispensing naloxone?	
Rules and reporting for pharmacists who are impaired or unable to perform functions?	
Requirements for retrospective pharmacist review?	
State laws surrounding drugs for "office use only"?	

Multiple Choice Question Self-Assessment

1. What is the primary objective of the Vaccines for Children Program?

A. Provide vaccines to pediatric clinics at cost
B. Mandate vaccines of highly communicable diseases
C. Provide free vaccines to uninsured or underinsured children
D. Incentivize pharmaceutical manufacturers to develop new vaccines for pediatric patients

2. One of your colleagues was recently exposed to a hazardous chemotherapeutic agent. Which federal agency creates standards and guidelines surrounding the handling of hazardous agents by healthcare professionals?

A. CMS
B. FDA
C. NIH
D. OSHA

3. Which of the following best describes the primary purpose of Phase 3 clinical trials in drug development?

A. To assess the safety and efficacy of a drug in a larger group of patients with the disease
B. To assess the safety of a drug in a small group of healthy patients
C. To assess the long-term adverse effects in patients who have taken the medication for over 5 years
D. To assess for rare adverse effects

4. When a manufacturer is looking to begin to give a new drug to human subjects, which application would be most appropriate to submit to the FDA?

A. ANDA
B. NDA
C. IND
D. SNDA

5. When a manufacturer submits an NDA, they can choose numerous different types. With a totally new molecular entity, what type of NDA should be submitted?

A. Type 1
B. Type 2
C. Type 3
D. Type 4

6. Which of the following statements best describes the FDA's Fast Track program?

A. The Fast Track program allows for a quicker recognition of serious adverse effects that may necessitate boxed warnings and removal of medications from the market
B. A program that provides quicker approval of medications for rare conditions affecting less than 1 out of 200,000 patients
C. A program that allows for the importation of non-FDA approved medications from other countries for rare conditions
D. The Fast Track program is a program that allows for a quicker review and approval process of drugs for serious or life-threatening conditions

7. In a hypothetic situation, the FDA has recently received an application for a new medication that works via the same mechanism as PPIs. The chemical structure is slightly different from lansoprazole. What is the classification that the FDA would place on this medication?

A. Fast Track
B. P Drug
C. S Drug
D. Q Drug

8. Which of the following is false with regards to the MedWatch Program?

A. It is under the umbrella of the FDA
B. Healthcare professionals are mandatory reporters
C. Form 3500 is the standard reporting form for healthcare professionals
D. MedWatch helps ensure the safe use of medications

9. Which type of FDA drug recall requires the swiftest action by a pharmacist/pharmacy?

A. Class 1
B. Class 2
C. Class 3
D. Class X

10. When a medication has a rating in the Orange Book, what does this designation indicate?

A. How effective the medication is for a given indication
B. It provides a risk versus benefit calculation number based upon the clinical literature
C. The bioequivalence of a medication compared to the reference listed drug
D. The comparative effectiveness of biologic agents in a given drug class

11. Which of the following designations in the Orange Book refers to an aerosolized solution?

A. AN
B. AO
C. AP
D. AT

12. The 1938 Food, Drug, and Cosmetic Act was passed to help ensure _____ of new medications prior to the sale and marketing of those medications.

A. Efficacy
B. Safety
C. Potency
D. Accuracy

13. The Hatch-Waxman Act helped reduce costs by which method?

A. Creating Medicare prescription drug plans
B. Regulating insurance companies
C. Allowing for interstate commerce of prescription drugs
D. Creating an easier process for generic medications to obtain approval

14. Which of the following would represent a schedule 5 controlled substance under federal law?

A. Triazolam
B. Haloperidol
C. Buprenorphine/naloxone
D. Diphenoxylate/atropine

15. A prescription contains a DEA number for Dr. Douglas Michaels. The DEA number listed is BW1284728. Is this a legitimate DEA number?

A. Yes
B. No

16. Which of the following providers would be exempt from DEA registration for the prescribing of controlled substances?

A. A physician working in a rural health clinic
B. A physician who works in both a hospital and clinic setting
C. A physician who works in the Air Force
D. A physician who is an addiction specialist

17. Which of the following is true with regard to federal law and the electronic prescribing of schedule 2 controlled substances?

A. It is not allowed under federal law
B. There are extra requirements on the prescription (compared to a written prescription) such as the phone number of the nearest DEA office
C. States may develop stricter regulations
D. E-prescriptions expire within 5 days of transmission if not utilized by the patient

18. What is the DEA federal requirement for length of time that records must be kept in relation to controlled substances?

A. 6 months
B. 1 year
C. 2 years
D. 5 years

19. Under federal law, which of these situations would not be acceptable prescribing of a controlled substance?

A. A veterinarian prescribing alprazolam for a dog's anxiety
B. A primary care provider writing a prescription for 10 oxycodone for office use
C. A dentist prescribing oxycodone for tooth pain
D. A nurse practitioner writing a prescription for naloxone

20. A patient has brought in a written morphine prescription for knee pain. It is deemed to be a legitimate prescription. The pharmacist fills the prescription and the patient refuses it because the cost is too expensive. They believe they can get it cheaper elsewhere. They have not paid for the prescription and it has not been dispensed to the patient. They would like their prescription back to go to another pharmacy. Under federal law, what should you do?

A. Call the physician for a new prescription that the patient can pick up at their office
B. Inform the patient that since it was put into your computer system, you cannot return the written prescription
C. Contact local law enforcement for further guidance
D. Give the patient the prescription and let them go to another pharmacy

21. Your pharmacy does not have enough hydromorphone to fulfill an entire prescription of 45 for a patient. You are able to dispense 30 tablets to the patient. How much time does the pharmacy have to fill the remaining 15 tablets?

A. 24 hours
B. 72 hours
C. 7 days
D. The remaining quantity cannot be filled in this situation

22. Federal law states that at a minimum, a full inventory of controlled substances within a pharmacy should be conducted how often?

A. Every month
B. Every 6 months
C. Every year
D. Every other year

23. Under federal law, when doing a controlled substance inventory, an exact count is needed for which of the following scheduled drugs?

A. Schedule 2
B. Schedule 3
C. Schedule 2 and 3
D. All Controlled Substances

24. If the DEA is planning to reschedule cyclobenzaprine as a schedule 5 controlled substance on December 31st of this year, when does federal law require a pharmacy to do an inventory?

A. 30 days prior to the anticipated date of schedule change
B. The day of the schedule change
C. Within 1 month of the schedule change
D. On the next routine inventory count

25. Which DEA form is utilized for loss or theft of controlled substances?

A. 41
B. 106
C. 222
D. 224

26. Which DEA form is utilized for the destruction of controlled substances?

A. 41
B. 106
C. 222
D. 224

27. What is the maximum amount of pseudoephedrine that may be purchased by one person in a day?

A. 3.6 grams
B. 7.5 grams
C. 9 grams
D. 18 grams

28. Which of the following information does not need to be obtained according to the DEA when someone purchases pseudoephedrine?

A. Date of birth
B. Address
C. Date of sale
D. Signature

29. What statement is true regarding USP?

A. It is a for-profit organization
B. It is run by the FDA
C. USP creates standards for the quality and production of medicines

D. USP creates and approves package inserts for all medicines

30. Per USP 795 Beyond Use Date recommendations, an oral, water containing compound should be stored under refrigerated conditions for a maximum of how many days before discarded (unless there is literature to support an alternative beyond use date)?

A. 1 day
B. 7 days
C. 14 days
D. 30 days

31. For employees of a hospital pharmacy performing sterile compounding, what is the minimum requirement for frequency of media fill testing recommended by USP for low risk preparations?

A. Every 6 months
B. Every year
C. Every other year
D. There are no recommendations for low risk preparations

32. When a manufacturer places an expiration date of 11/2028 on a pill bottle, what does this mean?

A. The medication will expire on the last day of November in 2028 as long as the bottle remains unopened in which case, it will expire in 6 months from the date of opening
B. It will expire on the last day of November 2028 regardless of whether the bottle was opened or not
C. It will expire on the last day of October 2028
D. Oral medications should be removed from inventory 2 years from the date received regardless of expiration date

33. You work in hospital setting that repackages medications for unit dose purposes. Which of the following would not be a requirement for the labeling of these repackaged medications?

A. Amount contained within the unit dose package
B. Lot number
C. Manufacturer or distributor identifier
D. Auxiliary labels for nursing administration information (i.e. take with a full glass of water)

34. Which piece of information is NOT required on the label of over-the-counter medications?

A. Intended use or indication
B. Patient warnings/instructions
C. Manufacturer information
D. Pharmacokinetics

35. The middle four digits in an NDC code represent which of the following?

A. The manufacturer of the product
B. Expiration date
C. Package size
D. The medication and dose

36. A pharmacy was destroyed by a hurricane. Any medications within that pharmacy would be classified as which term?

A. Adulterated
B. Misbranded
C. Inactivated
D. Illegal

37. As a pharmacist in charge, who will be the primary agency that you will report to regarding the licensing of your pharmacy?

A. FDA
B. USP
C. OSHA
D. State board of pharmacy

38. Which federal legislation enhanced pharmacist counseling requirements?

A. FDCA
B. OBRA 90

C. Hatch Waxman amendments

D. Kefauver-Harris amendment

39. Under federal law, what is outlawed with regard to self-prescribing?

A. Federal law bans self-prescribing outright

B. Federal law does not give any guidance on the legality of self-prescribing

C. Federal law outlaws self-prescribing of schedule 2 controlled substances

D. Federal law outlaws self-prescribing of all controlled substances

40. What is the name for an arrangement between a provider or group of providers and a pharmacist that allows a pharmacist to perform specific delegated patient care functions such as ordering new medications, changing medication dosages, and ordering labs?

A. Scope of Practice

B. Comprehensive Medication Review

C. Collaborative Practice Agreement

D. Credentialing and Privileging

41. Which application should be submitted for a new biologic agent used to target lymphoma?

A. NDA

B. BLA

C. DMEPA
D. ANDA

42. Years ago, the antidepressant named Brintellix was changed to Trintellix. Which agency would be responsible for monitoring the safety of names, labels, and packaging?

A. VAERS
B. CBER
C. NCQA
D. DMEPA

43. What is the purpose of a REMS program?

A. Reduce the risk of serious adverse effects or reactions
B. Ensure cost-effective drug therapy is selected
C. Study the safety of a drug in pregnancy
D. Maximize the benefits of medication

44. In the creation of a REMS program, which of the following is true?

A. The FDA sets up the program and the pharmaceutical manufacturer agrees to the requirements
B. Once set up, a REMS program is required forever as long as the medication is still being marketed and sold
C. A medication guide must be given to the patient

D. The program is designed to minimize excessive costs to the patient

45. How long is a schedule II prescription valid after it has been partially filled for a LTCF patient?

A. 30 days from the issue date
B. 14 days from the written date
C. 60 days from the issue date
D. 90 days from the last fill

46. What are the different ways a provider can send a schedule II-controlled substance prescription for a patient who is on hospice?

A. By email
B. Written prescription
C. By fax
D. B&C

47. For which of the following situations is a faxed schedule 2 prescription allowed?

A. A 4 year old with cancer
B. A patient who broke their hip and is in severe pain
C. A patient who resides in a long term care facility
D. A patient enrolled in Medicare

48. How long does a newly eligible patient have to enroll in a Medicare Part D plan?

A. 1 year
B. 7 months
C. 6 months
D. 3 months

49. Which of the following tasks would not typically be associated with the FDA's role?

A. Approval of REMS programs
B. Developing and creating compounding standards
C. Determining whether a drug requires a boxed warning
D. Issuing an alert on a medication safety-related issue

50. What piece of legislation set up two categories of drugs (legend and over-the-counter)?

A. Durham Humphrey
B. Kefauver Harris
C. Orphan Drug Act
D. Prescription Drug Marketing Act

Self-Assessment Answers

1. Answer – C
The Vaccines for Children Program is designed to provide vaccines to children who cannot afford them or may be unlikely to be able to afford them. This program has aided in the ability to increase vaccination rates. It is funded through the federal government.

2. Answer – D
OSHA (Occupational Safety and Health Administration) is the federal agency that sets standards and guidelines in relation to worker (healthcare) safety. Needlesticks, chemical exposure, hazardous pharmaceuticals, and workplace safety would all fall under the umbrella of OSHA.

3. Answer – A
Phase 3 clinical trials assess the efficacy and safety of a medication in a larger group of patients who have the disease.

4. Answer – C
An IND is an application for an investigational new drug. An Abbreviated New Drug Application (ANDA) is for the approval of a generic medication. An NDA is a New Drug Application that the FDA requires immediately prior to approval of a new medication. An SNDA is a Supplemental New Drug Application that may be submitted when a manufacturer would like to change the labeling of its medication.

5. Answer – A
A Type 1 NDA is one that is intended for a new molecular entity. Type 2 is for a new active ingredient (usually the change of a salt form). Type 3 NDA involves a previously approved medication that has a new dosage form for approval. Type 4 is a combination agent seeking approval. Both drugs in the combination need to be previously approved.

6. Answer – D
The Fast Track program from the FDA places an emphasis on prioritizing the review of drugs for serious or life-threatening conditions.

7. Answer – C
The "S" drug classification is selected by the FDA for drugs that have a similar molecule to an already approved FDA drug. "P" drugs - the FDA chooses this classification when a drug is a novel treatment or has advantages over existing treatments.

8. Answer – B
The MedWatch program is NOT mandatory. This program helps ensure safety of medications by allowing patients, consumers, and healthcare professionals the ability to report serious adverse reactions or problems with medications, biologics, devices, or dietary supplements.

9. Answer – A
A class 1 recall is the most serious medication recall that can be given by the FDA. The possibility exists for immediate danger, death, or injury. Action should be taken right away and drugs need to be prevented from reaching the patient. It is rare for this type of recall to happen. Class 3 is the least serious and Class X does not exist.

10. Answer – C
The Orange Book gives ratings for medications based upon the bioequivalence of the drug compared to the reference listed drug. This list of medications is managed by the FDA on all approved drugs.

11. Answer – A
AN is the abbreviation used in the Orange Book for an aerosolized solution or powder. AO is an injectable oil solution. AP refers to aqueous solutions. AT refers to topical products.

12. Answer – B
The 1938 FDCA allowed for increased factory inspections as well as requiring evidence that medications were deemed reasonably safe prior to the sale and marketing of those products.

13. Answer – D
The Hatch-Waxman Act made it easier for generic manufacturers to get into the market and drive down the costs of medications. It essentially allowed generic drug makers to only have to prove bioequivalence to the branded product.

14. Answer – D
Triazolam is a scheduled 4 controlled substance while Suboxone is schedule 3. Lomotil (diphenoxylate/atropine) is a schedule 5 controlled substance under federal law while haloperidol is not a controlled substance.

15. Answer – B (No)
Before you even need to add the digits up and do the math, the second letter should represent the first letter of the prescriber's last name. The 2nd letter is W and the physician's last name starts with an "M" so this would be an invalid DEA number for this provider.

16. Answer – C
A physician in the Air Force may be exempt from DEA registration. The other providers would not be exempt from having a DEA number. Army, Navy, Marine Corps, Coast Guard, Public Health Service, and Bureau of Prisons service may be exempt. They must however have a service ID number and state the type of service they are working in on the prescription.

17. Answer – C

States may develop stricter regulations with regard to the E-prescribing of schedule 2 controlled substances. E-prescribing is allowed under federal law and requirements for information on the prescription are going to be similar to a written prescription under federal law.

18. Answer – C
The DEA requirements for the length of time that controlled substance records need to be kept is 2 years. Legal counsel and state laws may dictate longer periods of time.

19. Answer – B
A prescription for a controlled substance supply delivered to a provider for purposes of dispensing to patients is NOT allowed. All of the other of the other prescriptions would be acceptable under federal law.

20. Answer – D
The patient has a right to their own prescription as long as the prescription has not been filled and dispensed to the patient. Under federal law, it may be returned to them.

21. Answer – B
If there is low inventory of a controlled substance, the pharmacy may fill the prescription with a partial amount and fill the remaining quantity within 72 hours. If the remaining quantity is not obtained within that timeframe, a new prescription will be required.

22. Answer – D
Federal law states at a minimum, inventory should be performed on an every other year basis. If an inventory is done on January 31st 2023, it would need to be done again on or before January 30th 2025.

23. Answer – A

C3-C5 controlled substances can be estimated as long as package size is 1,000 or less. An exact count is necessary when performing a schedule 2 controlled substance inventory.

24. Answer – B
In the event a drug becomes a scheduled substance, the day it becomes scheduled, an inventory must be done (tramadol, for example, was changed years ago from a traditional prescription medication to a controlled substance).

25. Answer – B
Form 106 should be utilized to report a loss or theft of controlled substances. The DEA states that "significant losses" should be reported but does not provide specifics on what that quantity amount or percentage of loss should be to be "reportable". It should be reported to the nearest DEA field office.

26. Answer – A
Form 41 is used for the destruction of controlled substances. The destruction should be witnessed by at least two people who shall be a pharmacist, physician, mid-level practitioner, nurse, or law enforcement.

27. Answer – A
No more than 3.6 grams of pseudoephedrine can be purchase in one day. The maximum for 30 days is 9 grams unless you are using mail-order which has a maximum of 7.5 grams per 30 days.

28. Answer – A
The date of birth of the patient is not necessary in the log book of pseudoephedrine sales. A photo ID should be presented and verified. Name, address, date and time of sale, and signature are all requirements. Date of birth is not.

29. Answer – C
United States Pharmacopeia is a nonprofit organization that creates standards for the quality and production of medicines. In relation to pharmaceuticals, its goal is to ensure that public health is maintained by ensuring the quality and safety of medicines.

30. Answer – C
Water containing oral compounds that are stored under refrigerated conditions have a 14-day maximum BUD or earlier BUD if one of the components expires sooner. ANY water in any component or the addition of water will fall into this category.

31. Answer – B
A media fill test (or aseptic manipulations skills) is a test done to prove that no contamination has taken place during the drug preparation phase. It is recommended to do this at least yearly for low to medium risk preparations. Individual states and institutions may have more strict policies based upon the IV services they provide.

32. Answer - B
If the expiration date does not list a day, it is assumed to be the last day of the month. Under normal storage conditions in a pharmacy, the date of opening should not alter the expiration of the medication for most medications.

33. Answer – D
Name of drug, amount, lot, expiration, identifier, and supplemental information such as exposure risks or refrigeration would all be required when labeling unit doses. Auxiliary labels such as those for patients on prescription bottles would not be necessary.

34. Answer – D

Pharmacokinetic information is not required by the FDA for OTC labeling. Pharmacokinetic information is intended for healthcare professionals and would likely be inappropriate for most patients. Product name, indication, manufacturer, amount, instructions, warnings, ingredients, phone #, and tamper proof seal are notable requirements for OTC medications.

35. Answer – D
The middle four digits are called the product code which identifies the drug product (i.e. 50 mg of tramadol). The first four digits are given to a company by the FDA to identify their products. This is called the "labeler" code (I.e. which company makes the product). The final 2 digits are indicative of what type of packaging the drug or product is contained within (i.e. 100 tablet bottle versus 1,000 tablet bottle).

36. Answer – A
Adulteration is defined as a drug that does not meet FDA standards in one of the following; quality, strength, or purity.

37. Answer – D
The state board of pharmacy is responsible for licensure and would be the agency that the pharmacist in charge should work with and report any changes to.

38. Answer – B
OBRA 90 mandated that a pharmacist must make an offer to counsel.

39. Answer – B
Federal law doesn't prohibit self-prescribing and does not have any specified limits. However, many states do have rules against self-prescribing.

40. Answer – C

A collaborative practice agreement (CPA) is a formal arrangement between a licensed provider (or a group of providers) and a registered pharmacist (or group of pharmacists). The agreement allows a pharmacist to perform specific delegated patient care functions. In general, most of the functions involve prescribing, changing medications or altering medication dosing. Examples include, but are not limited to, antibiotic dosing, warfarin dosing, diabetes management, hypertension management, or hyperlipidemia management.

41. Answer – B
A BLA is a Biologics License Application. This is the documentation and application submitted by a pharmaceutical company/manufacturer to get a biologic agent approved for sale and distribution in the United States. The CBER would review this application.

42. Answer – D
DMEPA is under the umbrella of the Center for Drug Evaluation and Research (CDER) and ultimately under the big FDA umbrella. The primary objective of this agency is to review medication error reports on prescription and over-the-counter drugs.

43. Answer – A
A Risk Evaluation and Mitigation Strategy program is designed to reduce the risk of serious drug reactions or side effects.

44. Answer – C
The manufacturer sets up the program and the FDA approves it. It is reevaluated periodically and may be eliminated or revised if new evidence on safety is available. Medication guides being given to the patient are required. The REMS program goal is to reduce the risk of serious adverse effects or reactions.

45. Answer – C

For LTCF patients, the pharmacy has 60 days to utilize that prescription. Once the 60 days is up from the original date, you may not dispense any more medication under that prescription.

46. Answer – D
For a hospice patient, it is allowable to utilize a written or fax prescription. Email is not allowable.

47. Answer – C
For patients who are enrolled in hospice or who are residing in a long term care facility, it is acceptable to fax schedule 2 controlled substance prescriptions.

48. Answer: B
New enrollees have 7 months to enroll during the initial enrollment period

49. Answer – B
The FDA doesn't typically develop and create compounding standards. This would be more of a task related to USP. The FDA may regulate pharmacies that do these activities, but they don't actually create the standards that need to be followed.

50. Answer – A
The Durham Humphrey Amendment was set up to create two categories of medicines. The Amendment set up a category of drugs that cannot be safely used without medical supervision and sale is restricted to a prescription (legend or prescription drugs). In addition, this legislation set up a category of drugs that could be reasonably used without provider supervision (over-the-counter or OTC's).

Did you find this review helpful? If so, I'd love a rating and review on Amazon! Thanks in advance! – Eric Christianson, PharmD

Made in the USA
Las Vegas, NV
03 May 2024